JOHN RUTTER
TOCCATA IN SEVEN

MUSIC DEPARTMENT

OXFORD
UNIVERSITY PRESS

TOCCATA IN SEVEN

JOHN RUTTER

Bright and rhythmic (♩ = c. 136)

Manual

Gt. mixt. *f non legato*

Pedal

marcato

Printed in Great Britain

OXFORD UNIVERSITY PRESS, MUSIC DEPARTMENT, GREAT CLARENDON STREET, OXFORD OX2 6DP

Reproduced and printed by
Halstan & Co. Ltd., Amersham, Bucks., England

OXFORD

Ophelia, Caliban, and Miranda

Bob Chilcott

for SATB, piano, and optional saxophone, bass, and drum kit

Saxophone, Bass, and Drum Kit part

The saxophone, bass, and drum parts may be played as written or used as a guide from which the player may improvise freely.

This part was prepared by Alexander Hawkins.

Duration: *c.*11 minutes

Bb/Eb SAXOPHONE*, BASS, and DRUMS†

Commissioned by picfest (Pacific International Choral Festivals), Peter Robb, Artistic Director,
for performance in Eugene, Oregon on 26 June 2016 by the Festival Chorus and the Yellowjackets

Ophelia, Caliban, and Miranda

1. River Bride
(Ophelia)

BOB CHILCOTT

*The saxophone part is presented at concert pitch, leaving players free to transpose for Bb or Eb saxophone.
†Drums *ad lib.* unless otherwise indicated.

OXFORD UNIVERSITY PRESS, MUSIC DEPARTMENT, GREAT CLARENDON STREET, OXFORD OX2 6DP